Women in leadership:

Empowering Female Leaders: Unveiling Strategies for Self-Confidence, Effective Communication, and Team Success"

Sharon D. Higham

All right reserved. No part of this publication may be reproduced, distributed or transmitted in any form or by any means, including photocopying, recording or other electronic or mechanical methods, without the prior written permission of the publisher, except in the brief quotations embodied in critical reviews and certain other non commercial uses permitted by copyright law

Copyright © by Sharon D. Higham 2024

Table of content

Introduction

Chapter 1:Leadership Terrain

Chapter2:Developing Confidence and Self-Discovery

Crucial Competencies for Successful Female Leadership

Chapter 3:Strategies for Team Management

Chapter 4:Mastery of Communication

Communicating During Meetings: Overcoming Communication that Apologizes:

Chapter 5:Facing and Overcoming Your Fears

Creating Boundaries Using a Four-Step Process

Chapter 6:The Basis for Successful Business Enterprises:

Chapter 7:Accepting Leadership; Gaining Knowledge from Promising Women

Introduction

Women are increasingly assuming leadership positions across a wide range of disciplines and businesses in the last several years. The increasing number of women in leadership roles is a result of continuous efforts to advance gender equality and women's empowerment in society. Although it is heartening to witness an increasing number of women shattering the glass ceiling, women's paths to leadership are frequently paved with difficulties and roadblocks.

For many years, people have debated the idea of women in leadership roles from a variety of angles. While some see it as a move in the right direction toward gender equality, others doubt women's capacity to manage and lead teams effectively. On the other hand, studies have demonstrated that women in leadership roles can lead their businesses to success and achieve positive change, diversity, and inclusivity.

It's critical to recognize and resolve the particular difficulties that women in leadership positions encounter if we are to fully realize the potential of female leaders. "Empowering Female Leaders: Unveiling Strategies for Self-Confidence, Effective Communication, and Team Success" is the discussion's focus in light of this. This topic will examine methods to empower and assist women in their leadership journeys as well as the essential components of female leadership, such as self-assurance, efficient communication, and team accomplishment.

Chapter 1: Leadership Terrain

A vital component of any society or organization is leadership. To accomplish the intended goals entails establishing a direction, persuading people, and carrying out plans. Throughout history, men have largely dominated the leadership scene. But things have changed dramatically in the last few years, with more women assuming leadership positions across a range of sectors and businesses. We will examine the state of leadership in a world where males predominate as well as the significance of women in leadership positions in this extensive subject. The State of Leadership in a World Rugged by Men Men have traditionally been seen as natural leaders, and women have been assigned to supporting positions for millennia. As a result, women now have to overcome several obstacles in their path to leadership positions. The term 'glass ceiling' describes an imperceptible barrier that keeps women from rising to the highest levels of an organization. This is frequently linked to pervasive discrimination in the workplace and gender stereotypes. Additionally, just 29% of senior management posts worldwide are held by women, indicating a deficiency of female presence in top leadership positions (Grant Thornton survey). As a result, there is an imbalance between genders in organizational culture and decision-making processes. Wayfinding in the World of Male Domination Despite these obstacles, women have persistently dismantled barriers and cleared the path for a more inclusive and varied leadership environment. Creating a support network is one of the most important strategies for surviving in a world where men rule. This may entail networking with other women in leadership positions or looking for mentorship. To combat gender prejudices and preconceptions also requires developing self-assurance and assertiveness. Promoting inclusive workplace rules and practices is another crucial element. Promoting women's responsibilities in both their personal and professional lives can involve creating flexible work arrangements and advocating for gender equality and diversity. The Significance of Female Leadership Positions The importance and influence of women in leadership positions are being increasingly acknowledged. Research indicates that the presence of women in leadership roles promotes better decision-making, enhanced financial outcomes, and a more welcoming workplace environment. In addition, female leaders are well-known for their capacity for empathy, emotional intelligence, and fostering long-lasting bonds—qualities that are essential to good leadership. Women also bring a variety of viewpoints and ideas to the table, which fosters creative problem-solving and imaginative thinking. Younger generations are inspired to break down barriers based on gender and follow their dreams through their presence in leadership roles.

Chapter 2: Developing Confidence and Self-Discovery

Accepting Your Leadership Journey: Accepting your leadership journey is a key component of self-discovery and confidence growth. Women are frequently socialized to be followers rather than leaders, which can impede their ability to advance personally. But it's imperative to overcome these restrictions and acknowledge that each woman can lead successfully in her unique manner.

It's important to take stock of your values, interests, and strengths before starting your leadership path. Self-discovery entails knowing your motivations and identity. It's important to acknowledge and celebrate any special talents and viewpoints you may have as a woman. You'll be able to lead with confidence and honesty as a result.

Having a good and encouraging network around you can also help you on your leadership journey. Look for peers, mentors, and role models who can motivate and inspire you. They can push you to move outside of your comfort zone and offer insightful advice and encouragement.

Overcoming Shyness: Lack of confidence can be a major impediment to self-awareness and confidence-building. Particularly women could experience pressure to seem quiet and follow social norms around what constitutes appropriate behavior for women. This might cause feelings of shyness in social situations, which can impede personal development and lead to missed opportunities.

It is essential to realize that shyness is a normal and common emotion that everyone encounters occasionally if they want to overcome it. Embrace your shyness and utilize it as a tool to better understand yourself, instead of attempting to repress it. To overcome your shyness and venture outside of your comfort zone, start small. This could include introducing yourself to strangers, signing up for a public speaking class, or engaging in activities that unnerve you. You will progressively gain confidence and understand that your shyness does not have to hold you back if you do this.

Imposter Syndrome: Women who experience imposter syndrome frequently and widely believe that their accomplishments are more the result of chance or other outside forces than of their talents and abilities. This can impede personal development and cause emotions of inadequacy and self-doubt.

Celebrating your accomplishments is crucial to overcoming imposter syndrome. Make a list of your accomplishments and consult it when you begin to question your abilities. Recognize that mistakes are inevitable for everyone and that feeling uncertain from time to time is natural. Instead of aiming for perfection, adopt a growth mindset and concentrate on ongoing learning and development.

Crucial Competencies for Successful Female Leadership

Any company or society that wants to succeed has to have effective leadership, and there has been a noticeable shift in recent years toward female leadership. Women are natural leaders because of their special talents and attributes, which include empathy, teamwork, and communication abilities. To be an effective leader, women must, like everyone else in a leadership position, possess a certain set of abilities and traits. We'll talk about the four key competencies for successful female leadership: fostering connections, enhancing self-worth, enhancing trust, and promoting inclusivity and diversity.

1. Building Self-Esteem: Self-esteem is the belief in one's value and potential. It helps women to believe in their abilities, which is crucial for effective female leadership. High self-esteem in women leaders increases their propensity to take chances, make tough choices, and defend their principles. Being at ease with one's strengths and shortcomings is essential to building self-esteem. It also entails learning to take criticism constructively and not take it personally, instead of

using it to make oneself better. By concentrating on their personal development, asking for criticism, and creating attainable goals, women can cultivate their sense of self-worth.

2. Honing Trust: Any effective connection, including that which exists between a leader and her team, is built on trust. Female leaders must hone their skills in creating and preserving trust with both colleagues and other stakeholders. This calls for acting with integrity, honesty, and consistency in both your speech and your deeds. Mutual respect and understanding are the foundations of trust, so leaders must pay

attention to and value the opinions and suggestions of their subordinates. Employees are more likely to be driven, involved, and dedicated to their tasks when they have faith in their leader.

3. Relationship Building: A leader must establish solid bonds with stakeholders and other leaders in addition to their team. Building and maintaining relationships is something that women are naturally good at, and this is a vital leadership talent. Empathy, attentive listening, and good communication are all essential to relationship building. Developing relationships and a rapport with people of different backgrounds,

cultures, and viewpoints is essential for a female leader. This promotes diversity and a pleasant work culture in addition to helping with decision-making.

4. Promoting Diversity and Inclusion: In the globally interconnected world of today, diversity and inclusion are essential to the prosperity of any group or community. You must support diversity and inclusion in all facets of your leadership as a female leader. To achieve this, hiring and promotion procedures must actively seek out and promote diversity. Additionally, team members must be encouraged to communicate openly and inclusively, and

a safe and welcoming work atmosphere must be established for all staff members. Women leaders can increase their teams' creativity, innovation, and productivity by appreciating diversity and fostering an inclusive workplace.

Chapter 3: Strategies for Team Management

A greater emphasis has been placed in recent years on encouraging gender equality and diversity in the workplace. As a result, there are now more women managing teams and assuming leadership positions. As more women occupy these roles, it's critical to create efficient team management techniques that play to their unique demands and advantages. We'll talk about some important tactics for female team managers to use in this article.

Establish an inclusive and supportive culture

For women to manage teams successfully, an inclusive and supportive culture must be fostered. This entails creating an atmosphere in which all people's opinions, regardless of gender, are valued and heard. Team members should be allowed to express their opinions and ideas and should be encouraged to communicate freely. Women will feel appreciated and able to meaningfully contribute to the team as a result of this.

Furthermore, team leaders must offer support to all members of their teams, particularly to women who frequently encounter particular difficulties at work. Be personable and kind, and when someone needs help, provide it. Everyone will benefit from a positive work atmosphere and trust will be strengthened as a result.

2. Welcome Differences

Diverse viewpoints, experiences, and backgrounds are a great addition to any team. Recognizing and valuing the diversity in your team, especially gender diversity, is crucial for leaders. Make sure that everyone's contributions are treated equally and encourage everyone to share their thoughts and opinions.

Women frequently bring unique viewpoints and skills to the table, and by recognizing and utilizing these distinctions, you can build a more cohesive and productive team. This fosters a more inclusive workplace culture and aids in dispelling gender stereotypes.

3. Offer Equitable Chances for Development and Progress

Ensuring equitable chances for training, development, and career advancement for all team members—including women—is imperative. In the workplace, prejudices and hurdles against women frequently impede their ability to advance professionally. It is your duty as a team leader to make sure that everyone in the team has equal access to opportunities for growth.

To assist women in gaining fundamental leadership abilities and to enable them the chance to take on difficult tasks and jobs, offer mentorship and coaching programs. Not only will this help each team member individually, but it will also help the team as a whole.

4. Use Effective Communication

Successful team management is based on effective communication, which is especially important when managing a group of women. Be clear about your expectations and provide your team members feedback regularly. Establishing trust will facilitate the development of a cooperative and efficient work atmosphere.

Don't forget to actively seek out the opinions of your team members, listen to them, and resolve any issues they may be having. Establishing a safe and open environment for women to express themselves is crucial since they frequently need to put in more effort to have their voices heard.

5. Set a good example
You have a special opportunity to serve as an inspiration to other women on your team as a female leader. Set a good example, exude confidence, and demonstrate that women are capable of assuming leadership responsibilities. This will help dispel any gender bias within the team and encourage and motivate the other members.

Additionally, recognize your prejudices and keep challenging them. Make a deliberate effort to provide each team member with a fair and equal work environment.

Chapter 4: Mastery of Communication

The ability to successfully express your thoughts, ideas, and emotions to others in a variety of contexts is referred to as communication mastery. It is an essential ability to have in both personal and professional contexts since it enables you to forge deep connections, work well with others, and accomplish your objectives.

We'll concentrate on two key areas of communication mastery: overcoming apologetic communication and speaking out in meetings.

Communicating During Meetings:

Meetings are a necessary component of communication in today's hectic work environment. They give people a place to express their thoughts, talk about tactics, and come to decisions. Public speaking and expressing oneself in front of a group, however, can be frightening for a lot of people.

Here are some pointers to remember to become an expert in expressing oneself in meetings:

1. Be ready: Before the meeting, compile all the facts you'll need and get ready to talk with assurance. This can entail going over the schedule, making notes, or running through your presentation.

2. Be succinct and clear: People's attention spans are short in meetings, thus time is of the essence. As a result, you must express your ideas succinctly and clearly. Get right to the point; don't ramble or stray from the subject.

3. Make use of non-verbal indicators: How you convey your message can be greatly influenced by non-verbal cues including keeping eye contact, utilizing hand gestures, and adopting a confident stance. These indicators show how self-assured and assertive you are.

4. Listen intently: Since communication is a two-way street, attentive listening is just as crucial as effective speaking. Be mindful of other people's viewpoints and give their opinions your full attention.

5. Make effective use of visual aids: Make use of any facts or images you have to back up your points. Using visual aids

can assist you in drawing in the audience and increase the recall value of your message.

6. Speak up: If there is anything you don't understand, don't be hesitant to add to the conversation or ask questions. Recall that you are contributing value to the meeting by speaking up and expressing your opinions and ideas.

Overcoming Communication that Apologizes:

The term "apologetic communication" describes the use of hesitant or unclear language, which can give the impression that you lack confidence and damage your reputation. Although it might seem like a harmless habit, constantly saying "I'm sorry" can make it more difficult to communicate.

The following advice will assist you in overcoming apologetic communication:

1. Recognize your patterns: Understanding when and why you apologize needlessly is the first step towards overcoming apologetic communication. Consider your language habits and note the circumstances in

which you most frequently employ words of apology.

2. Substitute apologetic language with assertive language: Try utilizing more assertive language, like "I believe..." or "In my opinion...", in favor of expressions like "I'm sorry, but..." or "I could be wrong, but..." You can come across as more certain and forceful by using this change in wording.

3. Use empowering statements: Saying aloud phrases like "I am confident in my ideas" or "My opinions are valuable" will help you feel more confident and less inclined to apologize.

4. Actively practice forceful communication: You can break free from your apologetic language habits by actively practicing assertive communication in regular discussions, even though it may feel awkward at first.

5. Have faith in yourself: Ultimately, having faith in oneself is the most important factor in conquering apologetic communication. Remind yourself that you are worthwhile and that you don't have to feel bad about voicing your opinions.

To sum up, developing effective communication skills is a continuous process. You can develop into a more proficient and self-assured communicator by putting the above advice into practice and consistently striving to make your communication better.

Chapter 5: Facing and Overcoming Your Fears

Humans naturally react with fear to danger or uncertainty. It's a strong feeling that can prevent us from realizing our full potential and accomplishing our objectives. It might immobilize us, making us reluctant to take chances and face difficulties. On the other hand, we will ultimately lose out on important chances and experiences if we let fear rule us. For this reason, facing and conquering our anxieties is a crucial skill for leading a successful and meaningful life. We'll look at methods for taking on obstacles head-on and turning fear into drive.

Understanding Fear: It's critical to first comprehend what fear is and its causes before learning how to face and conquer it. Our brains are designed with the natural survival instinct of fear to keep us safe from harm. It sets off our fight-or-flight response, readying us to either run from the threat or confront it. This impulse can become overly strong and make us fearful of non-threatening situations, which prevents us from taking necessary risks, even if it is essential for our survival in life-threatening situations.

Recognize Your worries: Recognizing our worries is the first step toward conquering them. Spend some time introspecting and considering the worries preventing you from reaching your objectives. List your anxieties and the ideas or preconceptions that go along with them. This will empower you to confront your concerns by assisting you in identifying their underlying causes.

Examine Your Beliefs: Irrational ideas and incorrect beliefs frequently serve as the fuel for our concerns. After you've recognized your anxieties, it's critical to question the veracity of these assumptions. Consider whether these views are based solely on conjecture or if there is any supporting data. To help you question these ideas and obtain a fresh viewpoint, you can also look for the assistance of a therapist, a dependable friend, or a member of your family.

Visualize Success: One effective strategy for overcoming anxiety and boosting confidence is to visualize success. Visualize yourself confronting and conquering your fear. Imagine that you are strong, self-assured, and empowered. When the time comes, you'll feel more equipped and inspired to face your concerns thanks to this.

Take Baby Steps: It can be overwhelming to confront all of our anxieties at once, and this frequently results in avoidance. Rather, divide your fear into more manageable, smaller steps. This will assist in de-stigmatizing the process and facilitate action-taking. Appreciate every tiny step you take and use it as inspiration to keep going.

Rethink Failure: The fear of failing can frequently be the source of fear. But it's crucial to keep in mind that failing does not define us; rather, it's a normal part of learning. Redefining failure as a necessary step on the path to achievement is crucial. Instead of using it as an excuse to give up, see it as a chance to improve and learn.

Seek help: Seeking help from friends, family, or a therapist is crucial because facing our concerns on our own can be challenging. Speaking with others about our anxieties can provide us with a fresh viewpoint, support, and guidance, as well as make us feel less alone in our efforts to conquer them.

Practice Mindfulness: Being mindful can assist us in controlling our fear in the here and now. Panic is brought on by our racing thoughts, which happen when we feel afraid. Deep breathing, meditation, and grounding exercises are examples of mindfulness practices that can help us quiet our racing minds and return our attention to the here and now.

Reward Yourself: It's critical to recognize and honor yourself for your achievements as you confront and conquer your fears. This will encourage you to keep overcoming your concerns and reward good conduct.

Creating Boundaries Using a Four-Step Process

In the dynamic and fast-paced workplace of today, establishing boundaries is crucial to preserving mental and emotional health. People may prevent burnout, boost productivity, and build positive relationships with superiors and coworkers by setting reasonable boundaries. Setting limits at work, however, can occasionally be difficult since it calls for a careful balancing act between professionalism and aggressiveness. Here's when a 4-step plan for setting up constructive limits at work comes in handy. This thorough tutorial will go over the value of establishing boundaries as well as the 4-step model's application to achieving a happy and satisfying work-life balance.

Why Are Workplace Boundaries Important?

Boundaries are concepts that pertain to the restrictions and guidelines we establish for ourselves in many spheres of our lives, such as our personal and work lives. Boundaries in the workplace are a vital safeguard against overwork, nosy coworkers, and hostile work environments. They support people in maintaining control, defining goals, and forming wholesome professional connections.

Without boundaries, workers are more likely to feel overworked, stressed out, and depressed, which lowers productivity and increases the risk of burnout. In addition, a lack of boundaries can breed animosity and conflict, which harms both individual well-being and the workplace as a whole.

The Four-Step Boundary-Setting Model

Establishing sound limits at work is a conscious, continuous activity that calls for assertiveness and self-awareness. The

4-step strategy offers a methodical way to assist people in establishing appropriate boundaries at work.

Step 1: Recognize Your Limitations

Determining your limits is the first step in establishing boundaries. Being self-aware and understanding what makes you feel comfortable and stressed out is quite important. You might need to impose restrictions on the number of hours you work, the kinds of jobs you accept, or the actions of your coworkers that you feel are inappropriate.

Step 2: Respectfully and Clearly Express Your Boundaries

The second stage is to politely and clearly explain your boundaries to supervisors and coworkers after you have established them. Without being hostile or submissive, use forceful communication to express exactly what you are and are not comfortable with.

Respectfully stating your boundaries is crucial for preserving positive working relationships with your coworkers. Recall that establishing boundaries is about taking charge of your well-being rather than about exerting control over other people.

Step 3: Maintain Your Limitations

Only when boundaries are regularly upheld can they be considered effective. Maintaining your boundaries and not allowing others to cross them without repercussions are crucial. Remind them politely of your boundaries and the repercussions of their behavior if they cross them. Enforcing boundaries consistently communicates that you take your limitations seriously and will not put up with boundary violations.

Step 4: Have a Professional but Firm Hand

Setting boundaries at work necessitates striking a balance between professionalism and aggressiveness, as was previously discussed. Setting clear limits is important, but you also need to communicate them professionally. Instead of being hostile or confrontational, speak with respect and keep your composure. This will support preventing disputes and preserving positive working relationships with your coworkers.

Establishing Boundaries While Maintaining Professionalism and Assertiveness

Striking the correct balance between professionalism and aggressiveness is one of the most difficult things when it comes to setting limits at work. While communicating your boundaries requires being forceful, going beyond can cause problems and strain relationships at work. However, being overly submissive might lead to people disregarding or undervaluing your boundaries.

Finding this balance requires that you know exactly what your boundaries are and how to respectfully and calmly express them. Keep your demeanor professional and remain receptive to constructive criticism and compromise from others. Keep in mind that establishing limits is more about taking care of yourself and making the workplace a happier place for everyone than it is about winning or being correct.

Establishing limits is essential to preserving a positive work-life balance and enhancing general well-being. To effectively express and enforce limits at work, individuals can follow the 4-step paradigm and strike a balance between aggressiveness and professionalism.

Reevaluating your boundaries frequently is important because your requirements and work environment can change over time. Establishing appropriate limits enables people to flourish on a personal and professional level, fostering a more happy and productive work environment for both themselves and their peers.

Chapter 6: The Basis for Successful Business Enterprises:

A brilliant CEO or a solid business plan are frequently cited as the cornerstones of corporate success. Even though all of these things are unquestionably significant, one vital component that is sometimes missed is your team. We will discuss the value of team dynamics and how cooperation may help your team achieve business success. Your team is the foundation of your company, and without a cohesive, motivated, and high-performing team, it is practically hard to produce remarkable outcomes.

Enhancing Collaborative Relationships:

The special interactions and bonds that exist between team members and affect how they collaborate to accomplish a common objective are referred to as team dynamics. The vitality, mindset, and actions of the group are what makes a team successful or unsuccessful. As a result, maximizing team relations is crucial to establishing a happy and effective work atmosphere.

Good communication is one of the most important components in optimizing team dynamics. Team members who communicate clearly and openly with one another develop mutual trust, understanding, and idea exchange. It is essential for a leader to create a culture of open communication and to support team members in sharing their thoughts and worries. This promotes the development of a cohesive team dedicated to accomplishing shared objectives.

Diversity is another essential component in maximizing team dynamics. Teams that are made up of people with different experiences, backgrounds, and viewpoints come up with new and creative ideas. The integration of diverse abilities and viewpoints facilitates problem-solving and decision-making, ultimately producing superior results. To fully utilize your team, it is imperative that you, as a leader, embrace diversity and encourage inclusiveness in the workplace.

Another important component in maximizing team dynamics is motivation. A highly effective team is driven. Establishing a culture at work that is upbeat, encouraging, and celebrates both individual and team achievements is crucial. Team members are more motivated to work more and provide better results when they feel valued and appreciated.

Reaching Exceptional Outcomes with Cooperation:

Working together to achieve a common objective is the process of collaboration. In the corporate world, teamwork is essential to attaining exceptional outcomes. It enables groups to optimize their combined skills and abilities by utilizing the individual capabilities of every team member.

Innovation and creativity are fostered by collaboration. When team members work together, they each bring unique viewpoints and specialties to the table, which sparks the creation of fresh, creative ideas. Working together on projects facilitates ideation and problem-solving, which produces solutions that are more effective and efficient.

In addition, teamwork cultivates a sense of accountability and ownership. When people cooperate and work toward a common objective, they take ownership of the team's success. Higher levels of accountability, devotion, and commitment to the project follow from this, and the result is exceptional performance.

Cooperation fosters growth and learning as well. It enables team members to impart their expertise to one another, which fosters the growth of new abilities and enhances output. In addition to fostering professional and personal development, collaboration allows people to gain knowledge from the experiences and viewpoints of their peers.

In summary, fostering cooperation and maximizing team dynamics are the cornerstones of corporate success. To achieve exceptional outcomes, you need a strong team that celebrates diversity, communicates well, and is driven to work together toward a single objective. It is critical for a leader to recognize the significance of team dynamics and to promote cooperation among team members. You may create a solid basis for the success of your team and, eventually, your company by cultivating a happy and cooperative work atmosphere.

Chapter 7: Accepting Leadership; Gaining Knowledge from Promising Women

A person with leadership qualities can inspire, encourage, and lead people toward a common objective. It is a crucial ability that is highly regarded in both private and public spheres. The value of varied viewpoints and views in leadership roles has come to be understood more and more in recent years. Consequently, there has been a great drive to embrace leadership and take inspiration from accomplished women who have had a big impact on their industries. People can develop the abilities needed to become great and powerful leaders by making positive changes toward effective leadership.

Accepting Leadership:

Realizing the value of leadership and its potential effects on people, groups, and society as a whole is the first step toward accepting it. Anybody can display leadership at any level, and it is not restricted to any certain role or position.

It's a way of thinking that entails being proactive, accepting responsibility, and motivating people to make great changes. To embrace leadership, people must push themselves to constantly grow and improve, venture outside of their comfort zones, and take on new challenges.

Taking advantage of leadership chances is one way to embrace leadership. This can be as simple as offering to lead a group or organization, taking on new tasks, or even coming up with an original idea or concept. People can improve their leadership abilities by actively looking for these possibilities.

To truly embrace leadership, one must also have a well-defined vision and purpose. True leaders are dedicated to a purpose bigger than themselves and possess a strong sense of direction. They strive to have a positive influence on their surroundings because they are motivated by their principles. People who possess a distinct vision and purpose are better able to inspire and encourage others and foster a sense of unity in the pursuit of a common objective.

Taking Advice from Women Who Achieve:

Glass ceilings and other obstacles have been cracked by women in a variety of disciplines and sectors in the modern world. The example of accomplished women in leadership positions inspires others, particularly young girls and women. Gaining knowledge from these ladies might offer insightful viewpoints on leadership.

Successful female leaders have a certain set of traits that have helped them succeed. Resilience, empathy, good communication, and the capacity to manage several goals are a few of these traits. Through seeing and gaining knowledge from accomplished women, individuals can cultivate these attributes and utilize them in their leadership endeavors.

The value of authenticity is among the most important things that successful female leaders can teach us. These leaders have succeeded in becoming powerful figures while upholding their moral principles. They are trustworthy and personable since they don't hesitate to be genuine and vulnerable. People may lead with integrity and influence and forge closer bonds with their teammates by embracing honesty.

Adopting a Positive Approach to Effective Leadership:

To be an effective leader, people must act purposefully and constructively. This entails assessing and enhancing one's leadership abilities constantly. The following are concrete actions that people can do to become effective leaders:

1. Lifelong Learning: Being a good leader requires constant learning. This entails looking for tools, seminars, and training programs to advance one's knowledge and leadership abilities. To find areas for growth, it's also critical to ask team

members for input and learn from mistakes.

2. Relationship Building: Skilled leaders are aware of how crucial it is to establish and maintain partnerships. To support team members in thriving, this entails actively listening, appreciating diverse viewpoints, and fostering an inclusive and friendly workplace.

3. Embracing Diversity: Adopting inclusive practices and diversity is a critical component of good leadership. To foster an environment where everyone can contribute and flourish, leaders must

recognize and value each team member's distinct talents and abilities.

4. Setting a Good Example: Successful leaders set a good example. This entails leading by example and serving as a mentor to their team members. Others are motivated to follow their example because they have high standards and hold themselves accountable for their deeds.

5. adaptation: Flexibility and adaptation are essential for effective leadership in the ever-evolving world of today. For their team and company to stay on course to achieve their objectives, leaders

need to be flexible, welcome change, and be receptive to fresh perspectives.

In summary:

For both professional and personal development, embracing leadership, picking up tips from accomplished women, and making positive strides toward effective leadership is crucial. People may motivate and enable others to realize their full potential by embracing leadership and never stopping to learn and grow as a leaders. We can create a world with more varied and influential leaders by adopting this mindset and strategy, which will improve everyone's future.

Milton Keynes UK
Ingram Content Group UK Ltd.
UKHW032116220224
438319UK00012B/846